Magic All Along

Cheyenne Bluett

ISBN-13: 978-1-7358649-6-9

BOOKS BY THIS AUTHOR

Poetry
His Green Eyes
Bright Yellow Sunshine
Dark Blue Waves
The Moon Sends Her Love

Paranormal Romance
(Pandora Bluett)
Wicked Transcendence

CHEYENNE BLUETT

DEDICATION

To the people who are doing the work to heal their inner child and make their life better. You are enough and beautiful, and I am so proud of you.

xoxo

FOREWORD

One day in therapy I learned about the inner child.

My therapist had brought it up
and recommended
that I should explore the opportunity to heal mine.
I'm always open to trying new things, so I agreed.

She then asked me to close my eyes and imagine
the little girl inside of me.
What does she look like? Where is she? What is she doing?
"Describe her to me."

Immediately I saw her:
Seven, maybe eight years old.
Blonde pigtails cascading around her shoulders
and wearing a pair of overalls.
She was sitting in a corner,
covering her eyes,
and sobbing.

My heart broke for the little girl
I recognized all too well.

She needed things
that she had never received
in twenty-five years.
Things that she still needs:

Love. To be accepted.
To know that she is actually enough
and exceptional just the way she is.
Above all,
she needs to heal from all the pain
she's been hiding inside.

And that's what we are here to do.

We won't heal it all in these pages
and it will take years and years,
and maybe more,
but here we are... working on it.

We must remember.
We must ache and resurface the trauma.
We must cry and yell and question
before we can finally breathe and smile and continue.

This is our healing journey.

Let us begin.

PART I

CHEYENNE BLUETT

From as young as I could remember
I never felt good enough for you.
I don't know what exactly caused it,
but it has been a feeling I've had my entire life.

Maybe it was because
you looked at me like I was a total inconvenience
when all I wanted was you to hug me.
Or the times you would complain
if I asked for your help.
Or the time you told me my sister was your favorite.
Or when you would ground me because I wasn't getting straight
A's.
Or when you'd call me stupid or ugly.
Or
Or
Or

I have what they call
"mother and father wounds."

My mother wound
makes me believe
I will never be enough,
and I people-please
to the point
of abandoning and betraying
my own needs
in order to be loved.

My father wound
makes me believe
I am unworthy of that love,
and I sabotage relationships
and then leave people
before they
can finally realize who I really am
(ugly, unlovable, stupid)
and inevitably leave me first.

Do I believe my parents
intentionally hurt me?
No.
But they didn't do the work
to heal their own pain,
so now I must have to,
and it's unfair...

I wish things were different,
but now all I can do is be better
for myself
and for my future children,
so they won't have to heal themselves.

I can do this for us.

You called it respecting you;
I call it fearing you.

Those are not the same.

"Stop crying or I will give you something to cry about!"
They said.

I would hope that you'd change if given the chance
and you'd undo all the pain you caused me...
but I've given you chances
to do exactly that,
and you're still the same.

I'm sobbing in the garage of my house
after you dropped me off.
I can't go inside yet because then
my mom would demand to know what's wrong
and I can't bear to tell her
what you just told me.

All I did was say goodbye to my sisters
and it triggered her
which triggered you.

You turned your entire body towards the backseat
and pointed your finger at me
and screamed.
"All you do is cause problems for me!
I hate you!
I wish you were never born!"

It's been thirteen years since that day.
My heart has never fully healed since.

You punished me
for acting like a child
when I was a child…

Every few poems I write
I have to pause from the tears in my eyes.
New memories appear
that I have pushed down for so long
and it breaks my heart all over again.

I'm so sorry, little me.

They said:
"Go ahead and tell people
about what I do,
and I will get out of jail
even more pissed off
and hurt you worse."

Why do my hands become clammy
and my heart anxiously beat
when you walk into the room?

Why do I still get flashbacks
when I hear someone
say your name?

What have you done to me
that makes me this uncomfortable,
so many years later?

Did you not want me
because of one reason,
or was it a collection
of all of my flaws?

What could I have done
to earn your love?

Love wasn't given freely in my home;
it was something you had to earn.

I didn't do it often.

Why would you make fun of me for being different?
I wanted nothing else than to be loved by you,
but instead
you always made me feel like an outsider.

No matter which house I slept at that night,
I was always the different child.
The intruder with two last names.

I was half her,
half you,
but I didn't belong anywhere.

SPL / IT

It is unexplainably frustrating
how you didn't love me
or take care of me
the way you should've
and the way I needed,
and now I need therapy
and medication
to feel like a "normal" person.

I am smiling as you talk to me
but you don't see me biting my tongue.

I am holding myself together
and keeping my emotions hidden
by tasting my own blood.

If you knew
the abuse I was enduring,
why did you continue putting me
in those situations?

Why didn't you
pull me away
from all the horrible comments,
nights spent crying,
welts on my body?

Why didn't you save me?

I remember being young
and seeing my moms friend at the grocery store.

We hadn't seen each other in a long time,
and she got so excited
she picked me up and hugged me tight.

I giggled from her enthusiasm
and felt overwhelmed with love.

Once she left, you sneered at me.
"It makes sense that she doesn't see you anymore,
because she acts like that when she does."

I was so confused by your comment,
and still am to this day.
What was so wrong about someone
being excited to see me?
Was I not worth a joyous reaction?
Why was/am I unworthy of love?

Some things are just too painful to write.

I learned at a very young age
that
in order to keep my family happy
I had to sacrifice my needs
and hide my true feelings.

But if they were happy,
it was worth it, right?

I'm crying in the bathtub
because of what you said to me.

My tears mix with the water,
staining what should be cleaning me.

I'm scarred by your words
and your hate isn't fading.

It's soaking into my veins
and searing upon my heart.

I was always erased
after every scheduled weekend with you
was over.

This is why I feel so easily replaced.

I was never important enough
for you to show up
to basketball games,
or scholastic bowl meets,
or anything in between,
but they were.

And it breaks my heart that you couldn't love me the same.

BLAME ME PART I

I was always blamed for things
that had no way of being my fault.

I guess it was just easiest to blame me,
since I was the odd one out.
No matter if I was 3, 7, 13, or 25.
I'm always the one who messes things up,
and makes your life miserable.

I remember having to shut down my emotions
to the point where I pretended
nothing bothered me
and I didn't care,
because I knew
that being numb
was better than
being berated or scolded
for crying
or being angry
or voicing my opinion
or showing any sort of emotion
that you didn't want to see.

Whenever something bothers me
I automatically snap at myself
"You're fine!"
instead of letting myself feel.

I am mimicking what I was taught,
because you never let me feel with you.

I always had to be *fine*
because being sad
or mad
or anything other than *fine* or *happy*
was wrong.

Home life spills into everyday life.
I'm starting to do what others want
to keep them happy.
Why should I fight it anyway?
Keeping the peace is way better,
even if I feel like I don't really matter.

I avoid eye contact
and look down
when people compliment me.

Even after all these years,
I still feel unworthy of praise.

Some days I hate looking in the mirror
because in my eyes,
the shape of my nose,
and the curve of my smile…
all I see is you.

I doubt my memories.
Those things didn't really happen, right?
That's just my imagination?

How could people ever treat me like that?
What did I do
to deserve the emotional neglect,
red handprinted tattoos?
The nights locked in a lightless bedroom
after being told I was just a mistake?

How could people
who were supposed to love me
abuse me?

You told me who I had to be
and forced me to live
how you wanted me to.

I grew up as another version of you.

If I had a time machine
I would use it to go back
and hug myself when I needed it most.

I would hold my little self in my arms
and promise her she'd be okay.
She's loved by people she hasn't even met yet.

"These nights are tough
but you are tougher
and someday you will know that."

I would remind her of her worth
and explain that
no one could take that away from her.

If I had a time machine
I would give myself the love
I never knew.

With every painting of my flesh
I would hear your words echoing in my head:

you will never be good enough
you will never be good enough
you will never be good enough...

Please don't be mad at me.
Even though I know
our fight is not my fault,
I'll make it right.

Just please promise me
you will still love me
even after my mistake.

How could you look

into her big blue eyes

and tell your eight-year-old daughter

you wish she were never born?

It was always
look at what she's wearing!
or
She needs to lose a few pounds.

Now here I am,
no longer a little girl,
but afraid of what you might say
if I ever end up looking that way.

I was called a "try-hard"
because I wanted to make sure
I did everything in my power
to have friendships.

Not knowing that I was projecting myself onto them
hoping to heal my wounds from home.

I was annoying and too much,
so no matter where I went
I was unloved and lonely.

No one to love me at home,
no one to love me at school.

I found solace
in starving myself
because it would make it easier
for me to hate myself.

I found solace
in reading
because it would take me away
from the loneliness.

I found solace
in self-harming
because punishing myself
was what I deserved.

I found solace in writing
because even if no one cared,
at least I could tell the paper how I felt.

I went through friendships and boyfriends quickly
because no one cared enough to stay.

It wasn't until I was older
when I met someone
who was a best friend and love all in one.

I married him.

And he loves me the way I always knew
I could and should be.
He listens to me cry and laugh and more.
He's always what I was looking for.

I remember when I told you
that something was wrong with me,
and I needed to see a doctor.

You rolled your eyes
and just said, *you're fine.*
Stop being so sad.
You just want attention.

I went back to my room and cried
as I picked up the familiar pair of scissors,
feeling even more alone
than before.

You invalidated how I felt so much
that now I don't even believe how I feel.
I constantly question my own thoughts
and fear making mistakes
with every decision I have to make.

Even the simplest things
like deciding where to go for dinner
send me into an anxiety attack.

I am so frightened of picking something
that the other person may not like,
so they'll get mad at me
or not talk to me again.

So I say, "I don't care!"
even if I do,

because me caring
could have
heartbreaking consequences.

Crying was a weakness
I wasn't allowed to feel.

I would tell you
you hurt me
and you'd only laugh at me
or call me a crybaby
or tell me to shut up.

Then you'd bring up my tears
and use it against me later,
and I just had to laugh
because *it was funny.*

(but it wasn't.)

You molded me into who you thought I should be
instead of allowing me to figure out who I was on my own.

The more I age and grow,
the more I struggle with who this person is.

Is this me?
Why do I believe X
and act like Y?
Is it because this is who I am
or because this is who I was forced to be?

When I take a step back
I feel incomplete, wrong.
Like someone else living in this body
that should be my safehouse.

Will I ever find out who I really am?
Or will I live my life
doomed to be
someone
who was *supposed* to be
someone else?

Being perfect
is unattainable,
so why must I pressure myself
to be the only person
in this world
who could achieve the impossible?

I remember one day
I did something that you didn't like
and you asked me how I felt.
I was honest,
and then you spanked me
four times in a row.
You asked me again
and I cried and I was honest
and then you spanked me
four times in a row.
You asked me again
and I cried and I was honest
but as you raised your hand
I quickly changed my answer
to what I think you wanted to hear.
You yelled at me
but didn't hit me again
and then you left my room
and slammed the door.

In that defining moment
as I sobbed on the ground
red and handprinted,
you taught me that my own feelings
do not matter.

Every time you told me
you wished I was never born,
a part of me
started wishing the same thing.

I never understood boundaries
because I wasn't allowed any.

My diary was read behind my back
and then brought up in conversation
at the dinner table.

My door was taken against my will
and I was refused privacy,
punished for one stupid mistake.

I was always forced to be an open book
without secrets or feeling different from them.

Tell me everything,
they would say.

If they found out
I ever kept something from them,
I was punished.

Why is it
the people who are supposed
to love me the most
make it seem
like I'm such a burden to love?

I would tell you that you hurt me
and all you'd do is laugh at me.

You were my biggest, meanest bully.

Even now, I'll bring up instances of when you hurt me as a child.

You will quickly defend yourself;
"That never happened! I never did that."

Well, you did.
You just don't remember
because it was just a normal day
and a normal experience,
while to me
it was life-changing
and trauma-inducing.

Don't try to tell me it didn't happen
because I've replayed it over and over
since the moment it did,
and you have never even thought twice about it.

Even as I try to remember everything that happened,
my mind comes up blank in a lot of memories.

I've blocked out your screaming,
the pain, the past, and your palms
because reliving it would be too painful to bear.

I am accepting
that somethings
I don't have to remember.

I can protect myself.

How could you put so much pressure
on a child
to make sure *you* were happy?

Why guilt her for being a child
or wanting attention
when you are her parent?

Why did you bring her into this world
if you didn't want to sacrifice for her?

Why didn't you love her?

Why make her feel guilty for
not trying to have a relationship with you
if you weren't trying either?

Why didn't you call?

Why did you yell so much?

Why couldn't you just hold her and tell her
it's okay to have big emotions?

Why did you make her feel like a burden for existing?

Why couldn't she be good enough for you?

All the questions I wish I had answers to.

CHEYENNE BLUETT

PART II

Writing out my story isn't fun.

It's painful.

But then I imagine
a similar soul
reading along
and feeling less alone,
and it makes it all worth it.

I will share my story
to save yours.

I never know the extent of my pain
until I casually talk to someone
and it is brought up
and they gasp.

My eyebrows furrow as they apologize for my past.

Oh wait... that wasn't normal?

Listen,
I know you're hurting,
but I can reassure you
you don't have to hurt like this anymore.

There is so much life left for you to live.

Close your eyes,
take a deep breath,
and imagine your future
without all this necessary pain.

You have the power to change your story.

Will it be easy?
No.
But will it be worth it?
Yes.

Why am I still trying to nurture relationships
that make me feel like garbage?

Why am I bending over backwards
for people who will never do the same?

Why am I loving a person
who has no ability to love me back?

When will I learn
that I deserve more than this?

I have always been told
I have an old soul
or that I'm mature for my age
and seem a lot older.

I used to take this as a compliment.

"Look how grown up I am!"

But now it makes me sad.
Looking back,
I never had the chance to
be *just a child.*

I was too busy growing up
so that I would be loved
by the people closest to me,
and taking care of
others around me.

I wish I would've been able
to be young, immature,
wild,   careless,   free...   the   way   children   should   be.

You used to say
that once I became a parent
I would understand why
you did the things you did.

Here I am,
now a parent,
and I still don't understand.

I will never, ever understand.

You do not get to rip apart my memories.

I have a right to say what I remember.

This is my pain,

let me heal from it.

I'm so terrified.
I grew up being taught
how to be the "right" girl.
I learned how to speak,
how to act,
how to be.

But now I'm realizing…
is she even truly *me?*

Am I who I'm meant to be
or who my parents forced me to be?
Who society wanted me to be?

Am I just a product of my time,
or genuinely this way?

I used to think I knew who I was
but now I'm changing
and it confuses me.

Things happen now,
and I react differently.
Things happen now,
and I feel differently.

I think back to one, three, five years ago
and can see how different I am
since being on my own.

I don't feel the need to stay in this cage I grew up in.

I want to break free, become the woman I'm slowly revealing...

but I don't know if I'm brave enough.

I am so quick to stand up
for a stranger
online or in person
when the size of their pants
is being teased
or made fun of
because size is unimportant
and doesn't define a person's character.

We all look different
and we are all beautiful.

But then
why do I cringe
at the number
on my own jeans at home?

I will reassure you that you're beautiful
but you'll deny my love
and point out
everything that is wrong with you...

not realizing
the things you hate
are also on my own body,
and you're only showing me
that I must not be beautiful either.

Reliving the hard memories
I've hidden away
has proven to be more difficult
than I ever could've imagined.

But as much as I don't want
to unlock these thoughts,
I know that
on the other side of these screams
is fresh air that I can finally breathe.

Why must my fear of loneliness
make me continue
to cultivate friendships
that leave me feeling empty
and unloved
and unheard
and worthless?

Starting therapy has made me realize
that I'm not broken.

I've always thought
there must be something wrong with me.

Why else do I feel this way?

But then she smiles at me from over her clipboard
and reminds me that
there's nothing broken about me.

My pain isn't my fault.
It's unfair that I have it,
and I don't have to hold onto it.

I'm not broken.

Let it go...

I've given you
chance after chance
after chance after chance…
and I'm realizing
that maybe I should stop
hoping you would change,
and instead start seeing you
for who you truly are.

Reminders:

You don't have to be perfect.

You are enough.

It's okay to say no.

You deserve to be loved for everything you already are.

Your body is beautiful.

This is your one chance at life; live it how *you* want to.

I promise it won't be the end of the world if you upset someone.

Your life is worth living.

I fear that my mental health issues
have been passed down to my daughter.
I worry about how she might feel,
what she might do,
if I ruined her before she even had a chance...

Then you remind me
we are not my parents.
We will be there for her
the way she needs,
love her more than anything,
and give her the best childhood we can.

I will give her the support
I wish I had.

I will be better for her.

Just because *you* never believed
You were good enough
or believed in *yourself*
or loved *yourself*

doesn't mean you can convince me
to feel the same about *myself.*

I am always so torn on what to do with our relationship.
Do I forgive you for the years of hell you put me through? Or
not?
Do I forgive you because I love you,
and that's what you do?
Or not?

I know you don't deserve it, but shouldn't I love you anyway?
But then, do I not respect myself if I don't just walk away?

I don't know what to do.
I can never figure out what I want to do.

I wish I had a clear, concrete answer... but I know one will never
come.

Becoming a parent
has really opened my eyes
and shown me
how bad of one you were.

I look at my daughter sleeping peacefully in my arms
and question how could look at me the same
and treat me the way you did.

I will never
ever
ever
treat my child
the way you treated me.

I wish I could go back
and cover my ears
the first time I heard
my mother complain about her body.

I wish I could go back
and cover my eyes
when reading a magazine
on how to lose weight.

I wish I could go back
and protect myself
from the feelings of unsatisfaction
when I looked in the mirror
and saw something different
than what was being praised all around me.

I wish I could go back
and erase the first thought
that started the idea
that not being a size 0
meant that I was ugly.

I will always be positive
and full of love
and kind to all the strangers in my life.

For someone to grow up
feeling as unworthy and unloved
and pointless as I felt,

It's the least I can do
in making sure
no one has to feel
the way that I did.

Even now I doubt my abilities
unless multiple people reassure me
that I excel in them.

I want to finally be able
to do things
without others' approval.

I was always told
my dreams were cute
but unrealistic.

I wish instead
that my gifts
were encouraged and praised.

Oh, how different things could've been.

Now here I am
trying to revive the momentum
of my passions
and banish all self-doubt
and fear of failure
to follow my dreams
and make them a reality…

while a wasted, half-finished college degree
sits collecting dust
in the rearview mirror behind me.

I know someone
tried erasing the magic
that lives inside you.

Don't let them convince you
that you are nothing.

You are everything.

My husband holds me as I cry into his arms.
"How could he have said that to me?"

He rocks me from side to side
as the tears stream down my face.
"Why wasn't I ever good enough for them?"

He kisses my forehead.
"I deserved so much better!"

He pulls my head up to look at him.
"Yes, you did. I'm so sorry.
But now you're here with me.
And I love you enough for all of them."

I always pride myself
in being the friend
that people come to
when they need advice
or help
or even someone to just listen
and tell them it will be okay.

Even though sometimes
their emotions and their life
are heavy on my heart,
I know that I am doing good
by helping others.

I just wish
that I had someone
like *me*
to turn to
when I need to.

You can't change a narcissist
or make them see the error in their ways
because
according to them
they don't have any.

Hard lessons I had to learn.

I am learning to accept people
for who they are
instead of me hoping
they'll be someone I need.

I'm learning who is a good friend
vs. one who says they are a good friend
and yet are never around when I need them.

I'm learning who to text with happy news
to get a positive reaction
vs. who would just one-up what I say.

I'm learning who to put my energy and love into
vs. who to let slowly fade away.

I love my parents.
I really do.
I know that these words
paint them in a negative light,
but I've forgiven them (mostly)
and we are still in each others' lives.

It's hard to explain,
and it doesn't make much sense,
but I'm sure you know
exactly what I mean.

I am teaching myself
that making a mistake
isn't the worst thing in the world.
Mistakes are how we grow.
Growth is good.
Mistakes = okay.

I remember the moment of realization
as if it were yesterday.

I was sobbing on the floor
and thought *this isn't right.*

I didn't want to continue
living my life like this
any longer.

I hated feeling like I was never good enough
and that my life had no meaning.
I had one-sided friendships
and I was tired of fighting for people
who never fought for me.
I kept seeking out emotionally available men
and were surprised when they didn't love me
the way I begged them to.

I hated my life and had no idea who I had become.
I needed more for my life.

I wanted to wake up in the morning
and be grateful for another day,
not dreading the fact that I was still alive.
I wanted to look at myself and be proud of who I was,
not continuing to hide behind everyone else.
I wanted to love myself
love my life
and live it according to myself,
not others.

In that moment on the bathroom floor
I finally accepted

that I deserved better.

And here we are four years later.

CHEYENNE BLUETT

PART III

It's officially been
over two years
since I've been working
on this healing journey.

I can proudly say
I feel so much better
and I've been doing the work
to change the course of my life.

Am I totally healed?
No.
I don't think I ever will be.

But here I stand tall
and proud
and *alive*
and know that
I am amazing.

I'm finally starting to believe it.

I cannot believe
I used to base my worth
on whether a boy
would text me back or not.

I am understanding
that the only reason you did
what you did
is because you never healed yourself.

A part of me feels sorry for you.
But the other doesn't.

You could've gotten the help
that I'm forced to now.

You couldn't been better
for yourself,
for me.

Now it's all up to me
to change the course
of our future family.

You make me feel something
no one has ever made me feel before.

This is how I know
you are the man I prayed for,
the one for me,
my soulmate.

How I know you love me
more than anyone else ever has,
and will love me more
than anyone else ever will.

You make me feel safe.

Finally.

It has proven to be a long process
but I am learning to trust myself.

I am no longer asking someone what they think
just to "double check"
when in reality
I need them to validate that I am right.

I am no longer asking someone
to make a decision for me
because I am too scared to make one myself.

After years of being made
to distrust my gut feelings or beliefs,
I am reminding myself
that I am smart.
I know what to do.
I can make my own decisions.

I look forward to the day
I can fully trust myself
like I should have all along.

When I found out I was pregnant
I was overcome with the fear
of being a parent.

I have always wanted to be a mother,
but how could I be the best mother
if I was still hurting as a child?

I was terrified to pass down my trauma
and continue the cycle
and bestow this unfairly painful life
to the baby I was carrying.

I looked at the sonogram picture
that had my little girl on it
and I knew that I had to be better for her.

I couldn't do to her
what my parents did to me.

I will heal my child
so that
I can give my child
the best life she deserves.

And I will heal my child
because I deserve
to live my best life, too.

I always find myself
focusing on the ones
who don't show up.

Why don't they care?
Why don't I matter to them?
Why can't they see how much they are hurting me?

And all the while
I am doing a great disservice
to all the ones
who are standing next to me.

I'm shifting my focus
to the ones who truly matter.

Cringing as I remind myself
I am enough
because my entire life thus far
I could never believe it.

It is taking a long time
for me to even
speak the words out loud,
but I am trying.

I am trying.

I've always searched for partners
who needed "fixing."

I loved the challenge of making someone better,
helping the ones who needed it most,
helping those in ways
I wish I had been helped.

That never worked out in the end...

Then I met you,
but you didn't need any of that.

For a while we struggled
because I was bored
from lack of toxicity
and petty fights I was so used to

but slowly I learned
this is what love should be like.

All along
you were the one fixing me
and I didn't even know.

I am so sorry
that your parent
made you feel
like you were a burden
just for existing.

I love you enough for them.

You are not a burden,
or a mistake,
or anything worse
they may have said.

I will love you instead.

Feel it seep through these pages
like a warm, cozy hug.

You were meant to be here.
I'm so thankful you are.

I worry that I chose the wrong path for my life.
Is this really what I should've done?
Would I be happier
if I had decided differently?
More successful?
Or worse off?

I can sit and wonder and dream about
the possibilities that won't ever come,
then I remember
there is never a *right* or *wrong* path.

There is only the path that I decide.

My life could've been
completely different,
but that doesn't mean
that it would've been better or worse.

I could've done everything differently
and somehow still ended up
where I am today.

With every choice I make
I change my life.
It's all up to what I decide.

So, who will I be tomorrow?
What life will I continue to create?

I can't wait to see.

I always wanted to fix our relationship.
I spent years trying to mend our bond,
and slowly gave up as more time went on.

Now that I'm a parent of my own...
I no longer have that desire.

I look at who I am to my child
and look at who you were to me
and cannot
for the absolute life of me
understand why you did what you did.

I will never be the parent you were
and you will never deserve my forgiveness.

And I'm finally
accepting of the fact
that you will never be the father
I always wished you would be.

I never thought I could love myself
the way you said you loved me,
but I took the time
to learn myself
through your eyes
and now I see
all that you do.

I love me
just as much as
I love you.

I look into the eyes
of the baby I created
and I see that she
inherited my eyes.

Which means
she inherited
your eyes.

But now
when I look into
these gray-blue irises
I don't see contempt
or disgust
or unworthiness.

I see love
and adoration
and connection
and belonging.

I see everything I had wanted
and wished for from you.

And I know that
when my daughter
stares back into my eyes,
she will be mirrored
with love and adoration
and connection and belonging.

As she should be.

It's so crazy
how I go to places
I have been in my past,
and while my life is so much better
and the days are so much different,
if I close my eyes
in this restaurant parking lot,
I can still hear you screaming at me.

I grieve for the relationship I know we will never have.
I understand that it is purely circumstantial—
if our childhood was different, we might've loved each other
more,
or become closer,
but now we are adults
who speak in passing
and love from a distance.

And there's nothing more I could've done.

Edit to add:

I wrote this while I cried about not being close to my sisters,
but I have put more effort in
and can happily say
that we talk every day.

It's never too late.

My bracelets scratched me
and left a line
that resembles the ones
I used to make on purpose.

I close my eyes and take a deep breath,
but I don't have the urge
to make any more.

I open my eyes
and continue my day
with a relieved, proud
smile on my face.

I never thought I'd get to this day,
but here I am.

I'm so freaking proud of myself.

Give yourself grace.
You won't conquer your trauma
and heal years of pain
in one day.

You won't fall in love with your changing body overnight.
You won't find the perfect medication the first time you try.
You won't move on from your unrequited love in seconds.

It will take time.
Lots of it.
Days, years,
maybe even more.
Is it going to be annoying
and hard?
Yes.
At times will you stop and think
"What's the point in trying this hard if it still hurts?"

But then you will have days
where you look back and see
how far you've already come
and you'll realize the only thing to do
is keep going.

Because you're doing the damn thing.

As I type this book
I realize
this year is
my 10 year anniversary
of living.

10 years ago
I tried ending my life
multiple times
because it was just too hard.

But here I am
still standing
(well, sitting)
and breathing
and living.

If I wouldn't't've been forced to get help
I never would've...

Wrote and published 6 books (and counting!).
Got married to the love of my life.
Made countless friendships with the most amazing people.
Had a baby.
Saw a shooting star.
Watched Twilight again and again.
Laughed until my belly hurt.
Ate the best chocolate chip cookies.
Realized I was enough.
And more...

I have done the hard job
of surviving,
10 years have gone by

and I am still alive.

Here's to the next 10!

I always believed I needed a partner to complete me.

I yearned to find that person
who would make me feel
desired, loved, enough.

Then I got married
to the man of my dreams
and I still felt unworthy.

What is this?
Where are all the feelings
I thought would appear?
Why do I still
have these negative thoughts,
believe these horrible things?

It took that disappointment
to realize
that no person
can make me feel those things.

I had to believe
that I was
enough, loved, worthy
just because I was.

I still struggle most days,
but I am learning in every new moment
and loving myself every step of the way.

I am unlearning
all the bad and the snide
and the rude and the judgmental
and the totally inaccurate things about me
that the people closest to me
imprisoned me in.

Who am I, really?
Without all those things?

I stand in front of the mirror,
ready to introduce myself
to the me I've wanted to be
all along.

It's nice to finally meet you.

I can remember our memories fondly
and still not want
to create more with you.

As I sit here today
it hits me.
I am sitting in the place
and living in the moment
I have always wished for
and looked forward to.

It may look a little different
than I had imagined,
and it may have taken
a few different routes
and detours to get here,
but I made it.

Here's your sign:

everything will work out. *I promise.*

Because of you
I let another man
yell and ignore
and treat me like you did.

I stayed with men
who didn't love me correctly
and called me names
and made me feel unworthy
because that's what I thought love was.

That's what I was used to.

Not knowing how wrong both of you were,
and how I deserve so much better.

I promise
to break this generational curse
that has been passed down in my family
far too long.

I will love my child(ren)
with every burning ember in my soul.
I will allow them to be emotional
and cry and scream and yell.
I will allow them to be honest
and not expect them to do whatever I want or say.
I will allow them to be who *they* choose to,
not who I wish they would be.
I will love and accept them
no matter who they become
because that's the absolute most important thing.

Don't nitpick who you are
because of someone else.

You may think they are perfect
and yearn to be like them,
but I promise
you are already extraordinary
in your own magical way
of being you.

to my love:

Whenever I feel
out of focus
I make sure to find you.

On those days where I believe
that this world would be better without me,
or the days I just want
all the pain to stop,
I reach out for you.

Your strong, unwavering hands
cling onto mine.
Your lips breathe peace
back into my heart.
You make me remember
who I am
(and that is not my trauma or illness).

You will always be the one
who can help
make me
myself again.

I am messy.

I have clothes strewn
around my house,
and torn notebook pages
stuffed in dirty jean pockets.

I don't brush my hair everyday,
and I have half-read books
on every table.

I cry when I'm happy.
I cry when I'm sad.
I cry when I'm angry.
I cry… a lot..

I laugh at the most inappropriate times.
I have people tell me they envy me,
yet they don't know
how much I struggle to look at my reflection.

I spend too much money
on stuff I don't need
and don't pay my bills on time.

I abandon a project
if I don't master it
within a few days.

I go to therapy,
I get high sometimes,
and I pray to a God
I hope
loves me as much as he promises.

I am a woman
filled with kaleidoscope colors
and bright yellow sunshine.

I am messy.
And I am me.
And I'm learning to love
every messy part of me.

I am calling back my power
by deleting all
my memories of you,
and replacing
these worn photographs
with happier snapshots of myself.

I am no longer apologizing to keep the peace.

I look back at all the times
I'd apologize
for absolutely no reason
and when I'd done nothing wrong
just so that
the other person
would no longer be upset.

I'm so done with that!

They will survive
if they are upset.
It's not my responsibility
to worry about their emotions.
I am no longer sacrificing
my own needs
and stepping over
my own boundaries
for another person.

It's time that other people
start apologizing to me.

If I would have succeeded
in ending my life,
you never would've existed.

I look at your perfect face
and wonder how this world
could've lived without you.

Spoiler alert: it couldn't have.

I'm so proud of myself
for pushing through
the terrible days,
cruel circumstances,
and horrible nights,
and still choosing to live.

Because every hard day
that I had to fight to survive
led me to you.

I always wanted to become the woman
who was strong no matter what.
The woman who never let anything get to her,
the woman who kept working hard
even though she didn't want to.
The woman who never cried
and who always held her head up high.

My life goals have changed.

I want to be the woman
who feels every type of emotion she needs.
The woman who takes breaks when she feels overwhelmed,
no matter if it upsets others.
The woman who says "no" without feeling guilty.
The woman who sobs when sadness floods her body.
The woman who brings other women up,
but also might need reassurance from time to time.
The woman who grieves death and change and more,
and who doesn't rush herself doing so.

I will be the woman who feels every negative emotion
and rests
and stops doing things that make her feel like shit.

I will never be consistently happy and I'm tired of apologizing
for it.

This is real life—this is me—and this is who I want to be.

I used to be so terrified of cutting you off
because I didn't want to hurt your feelings.

Screw your feelings.

You never thought about mine
when you stomped on my soul
and broke my spirit
every chance you could.

I know as I type this,
I am creating enemies,
but I do not care.

You should not have treated me the way you did.

You could've stopped it
or changed
but you didn't.

So here I am
exposing my pain
and annotating my journey
because if it helps
at least one other person
who is sobbing in their bedroom
begging to know
Why is this happening to me?

Then it is all worth it.

In order to fully love my body
I must accept
that the goal of getting
back down to the size I was
in high school
(and even smaller)
is highly improbably
and more than a little unrealistic.

I have to love my body
for who she is now,
and who she will be
the remainder of my life.

Curves, rolls, scars, marks, and all.

I'm sorry someone made you feel

shameful
stupid
or wrong

for having emotions.

You are allowed to feel

annoyed
heartbroken
outraged
ecstatic
and more

without any judgement.

I know this has been said
one thousand times
and will be said
one thousand more,
but here it is:

You are special because you are *you*.

Don't roll your eyes
or huff out a sigh.

It is so, so, so true.

The atoms and stardust
that flow through your veins,
combined with
your gemstone eyes
and your radiant smile,
the way you laugh
and all your dreams
make you the most
amazing person.

The most amazing person... YOU.

Sometimes I get so angry
at what my childhood was like.

My life could've been so different
if it was different.

But then I wouldn't be here
at 9:08pm on a Saturday night
writing these words
so *you* would feel less alone.

I wouldn't be as compassionate
or kind
or loving
or grateful.

And I know that
even though growing up
was horrible and unbearable at times,
I wouldn't change it for a thing.

Why must I always reassure myself
that I am good enough for this world?

Why can't I be proud of myself?

I want to scream from the rooftops
that I love who I am…

but it's extremely difficult.

You are allowed to do what's best for you.

I know you've been taught
to think about others first
and to keep the peace
no matter how you feel,
but now it's finally your time
to stop doing that.

Be selfish with your time.
Be selfish with your heart.
Be selfish and do what you want.

It will feel super duper uber weird at first.

You will feel guilty and wrong and mean.

I'm here to tell you—push through those thoughts.

I can see from the other side,
and it is nice and cozy and warm over here.

You can do it.

I am learning to let go
of wanting to control my life
and to trust the process.

I'm allowing my life
to do what it wants,
go where it's supposed to.

I'm continuing to work hard,
but no longer breaking my back.

I'm doing my best,
but no longer stressing over
the tiniest details...

My life will be
what it will be
one way or another.

I might as well
go with the flow
and find out my path,
instead of causing myself
sleepless nights
and drunken panic attacks
because I want to know *right now*.

Everything will happen
the way it was supposed to
from the very beginning.

I'm taking back my wish
to be liked by everyone else.

I don't need that anymore—
I only need to be liked and loved and appreciated
by myself.

For all the years
I would look at my reflection
and cry because my nose was crooked
and cry because my teeth were off-white
and cry because my body wasn't perfect,
I'm sorry.

For all the years
I would look at my reflection
and cry because I failed at something
and cry because I didn't stand up for myself
and cry because I hated myself,
I'm sorry.

For all the years
I would look at my reflection
and wish I were someone else
and wish I was different
and wish I was dead,
I'm sorry...

Now,
I look in the mirror
and smile.
I remind myself
I am enough,
I am strong,
I am beautiful,
I am loved,
and I am worthy.

Just the way I am.

You should never have to ask
for permission to be yourself.

If you find yourself doing so,
then those people aren't meant to be with you.

And that's a good thing.

Don't be afraid to reintroduce yourself.
They may have known you before,
but that's not who you are now.

They don't know the new you
who stands proudly before them.

The one who spent countless hours healing
and grew and changed in all the best ways.

Show them
and demand the respect
that you were once too scared to ask for.

Not everyone will like you.

It's just a fact.

Being true to yourself,
being happy,
and being inspiring
will upset some people.

Let them be upset!

Don't try to win them over
by making yourself smaller,
by people pleasing,
or by changing who you are.

<u>You are awesome.</u>

You will find the people who think so.

Don't be afraid
to feel your emotions.

Don't push away the feelings
you don't want to acknowledge.

You aren't a robot;
you are a living, breathing human.

Experience every feeling
that comes with that territory,
and give yourself
love and grace
as you do so.

I have learned
that being the bad guy
isn't always a bad thing.

I'll be the bad guy
if that means
I set boundaries
and I stick to them.

I'll be the bad guy
if that means
I don't show up to Christmas dinner
because I know they will be there.

I'll be the bad guy
if that means
I won't break my bones
and bleed for you.

Being the bad guy for you
is really
me being the good guy for myself.

Whenever I criticize myself,
you always object
and tell me,
"You're perfect."

I usually roll my eyes
and remind you that I'm not.

Now,
after my healing journey,
I realize that maybe you are right after all.

No longer am I the doormat
you so easily walked across
and scraped your dirty feet on.

Now I'm the door
slamming in your face.

You do not get to disrespect me ever again.

With every year that passes
I step even more
into the woman I am becoming.
I have changed so much already
in these past few years,
and with each passing sun
I become better and better.

I cannot wait to see
the woman I am next year
because I know she will be even more
happy, healed, and hopeful.

25.

I've been told countless times
that it's my responsibility
to forgive those who wronged me.

"It's because they were abused as a child."
"That's just how men are, they don't understand."
"She would treat you differently if you had been easier."
"They love you, even if it doesn't seem like it."

No.

It's not fair for people
to continue the cycle of abuse
just because that's what they have always known.

I understand that they are hurting,
and I'm sorry they went through that,

but *how dare* you push that responsibility on me?

I'm just a young girl.
I don't know any better.
Doing this to me now
will affect me the rest of my life...

Every time I meet a man
I will cringe when he moves too fast.

Every time I make a mistake
I can hear your disappointed scoff.

Every time I take a chance
I can hear your hateful voice
reminding me that no one cares.

Every time I ... *sigh.*

Will I ever forgive you?
I don't know.

I wish I could go back
as far as I have to
and heal the great-great-great grandmother
I never knew.

Things could've been different
if she would've known
how she should be treated
or how she could heal her pain.

And she could've spared her daughter
the same pain
and her daughter
and her daughter
and her daughter…

I wish my mother could've felt love
the way I am learning to love myself.

I wish my grandmother could've confidently said no
the way that I am learning to.

I wish all the women I am related to could have a do-over and
live her life for herself, not by appeasing everyone around her.

I wish that life could've been nicer or easier for them, but I know
all I can do now is pray they realize they deserve so much better.

And I promise that I will heal myself
so my daughter won't have to.

For once in my life
I love the sound of silence.

I love not having
to talk meaningless conversations
with people who don't even care.

I love saying no to things
I don't want to do,
even if it disappoints the other person.

I am no longer doing what everyone else wants
because I have these need to feel wanted.

I don't care about that anymore.

I'm enjoying living my life for me.

Boundaries.

My body is beautiful.
My body is beautiful.
My body is beautiful.

Even though
I don't 100% agree
with that above statement yet,
I know that the more I repeat it
the more I believe it.

I appreciate the gesture,
but you do not have
to tell me
how proud you are
of who I've become
despite all my circumstances.

I'm proud of myself, and that's all that matters.

No has become
my new favorite word.

I used to be terrified
to utter the sound,
but now I will say it
firmly and often.

No. Nope. No.

It's selfish of me to say this…
but I'm going to say it anyway.

You might still be alive,
but you've been dead to me
a long time.

Every time you broke me down,
the vision I had of you
died a little more.

Every time you yelled,
berated,
terrified,
abused,
beat,
laughed at,
and crushed me,
you died a little more.

Then when I'd forgive you
and you'd do it all again,
over and over and over,
you died and died and died.

Until finally, here we are.
I no longer have love for you.

But how do you grieve a person who's still alive?

I tried so hard
to make myself a copy
of people who always seemed
to be liked.

If I wanted to be liked,
I must act like *this*.

If I wanted to be funny,
I had to joke like **this.**

If I wanted to be pretty,
I had to do my makeup like <u>this.</u>

I focused so hard on being a person
everyone else would love
that I neglected to be a person that *I* would love.

I'm finally learning who I am beneath the faux me.

I'm a girl who loves oversized t-shirts
and drinking too much root beer.

I'm a girl who goes days without washing her hair
and loves to buy millions of scrunchies.

I love a good glass of wine
and either wearing no makeup for days
or going glam every day for a week.

I love staying home and reading a good book
but occasionally like to drink too much at bars.

I will post on social media

and then disappear for two months.

I'm funny in my own way,
and I'm pretty even though I don't look like them.

I'm nothing like the people
I thought I had to be like,
and even though it took me
until my mid-twenties to realize,
I'm happy I've finally
arrived at this place.

I have the rest of my life
to show off
this real me I've been hiding.

I do not have to see you anymore.
I am allowed to let go of friendships
that make me feel like shit.

I don't have to worry about
how you will act on Thanksgiving,
or what you will say
if I post a certain picture.

I can stop answering the phone
and responding to meaningless texts.

I don't have to do anything with you

and I don't have to feel guilty about it.

BLAME ME PART II

I was always blamed for things
that had no way of being my fault.

I guess it was just easiest to blame me,
since I was the odd one out.
No matter if I was 3, 7, 13, or 25.
I'm always the one who messes things up,
and makes your life miserable.

I am finally learning
that you have always been wrong,
and it has never been my fault,
and your anger
has never had anything
to do with me.

I deserved to be loved.

Not with conditions or reasons.
Not only if I did this thing,
or accomplished that.

I deserved to be loved
because I *just was*.

I have sunshine in my soul
and galaxies in my heart.

I know that I am worthy
and a precious piece of art.

I am beautiful and kind
and amazing and enough.

I can handle anything thrown at me,
painless or rough.

Now matter what you think of me,
I am sure of who I am.

You don't like me?
Good.
I don't give a damn.

I'm sitting here
in a coffee shop
with a delicious latte
on a warm sunny day,
my laptop opened to all my poems,
and I know that it will all be okay.

Here I am
living my dreams
with a screensaver
of my beautiful family
and a notebook filled
with all my future possibilities

Life worked out.
And I can feel the little girl inside of me
smiling as big as the outside me.

I have been told
that I radiate sunshine
and I make everyone around me
feel better, smile bigger
just by being me.

I have also been told
that I'm way too much,
and I am annoying
and I make people miserable
just by being me.

The moral of the story is
some people will like me,
while others will not.

And I will be okay

A letter to my daughter:

I promise that I will love you fiercely and make sure you never doubt it.

I will make sure you feel my love on each day you live on this earth.

I will love you for who you are and nurture you to grow into the person you're meant to be.

I will heal your big emotions with even bigger hugs and I will make sure my arms are a safe place for you.

I won't ever let another person lay a finger on you, or make you feel as if you aren't enough just the way you are.

If someone tries, I will remind you of your power, and how much I love you.

I will remind you of your beauty, no matter if you look like me or the magazines or neither.

I will be there through every heartbreak, every celebration, and every in-between.

I will never ever let you forget the magic that lives inside of you. But most of all

I will love you fiercely and make sure you never doubt it.

and finally...

To my inner child:

I am sorry you didn't receive the love you deserved.
I am sorry people made you think you were hard to love
or that you would never be good enough to love.

I wish I could rewind time
and make sure you knew how special you were
all this time, but I can't.

All you can do now is heal and love yourself the way you
deserve.

We might have started this journey,
but it is far from over.
It will take years, it won't be easy
(as you have come to find out),
but I know you can do it.

You are smiling more often,
and you are wiping away tears.
You can do this.
You can do this...

Remember you are more than enough.
Remember you don't have to be the person you were forced to
be.
Remember it's never too late to live the life you've always
dreamed.
And always,
always remember,
you are a person deserving of love.

Never forget, you beautiful soul,
that you have been
MAGIC ALL ALONG.

ACKNOWLEGEMENTS

Thank you to my husband for being my biggest supporter, my sexiest muse, and my best friend.

Thank you to my daughter who helped me realize I deserved more for my life, and I needed to heal so she could have the childhood I didn't.

Thank you to my therapist who has helped me on my healing journey, whom I probably wouldn't be alive without!

Thank you to my family for their love and acceptance of knowing how they affected me growing up, but also for vowing to change and be better for themselves and for me.

Thank you to all my best friends who support my writing and believe in me every day.

And last, thank you to my readers who let me have the coolest job in the world.

CHEYENNE BLUETT

ABOUT THE AUTHOR:

Cheyenne Bluett was born and raised in Illinois, where she still currently resides with her husband, fur-children, and human daughter. When she is not writing or working on one of her ten thousand projects, you can find her snuggling her daughter, reading a good book with a hot chocolate, or rewatching Twilight for the thousandth time.

CHEYENNE BLUETT

CAN YOU HELP?

Thank You For Reading My Book!

I really appreciate all of your feedback, and I love hearing what you have to say.

Please leave me a review on Amazon letting me know what you thought of the book.

Thank you so much!

Xoxo,

Cheyenne

Printed in Great Britain
by Amazon